ICE CREAM

Ivan Day

SHIRE PUBLICATIONS

Published in Great Britain in 2011 by Shire Publications Ltd, Midland House, West Way, Botley, Oxford OX2 0PH, United Kingdom.

44-02 23rd Street, Suite 219, Long Island City, NY 11101

E-mail: shire@shirebooks.co.uk   www.shirebooks.co.uk

© 2011 Ivan Day

All rights reserved. Apart from any fair dealing for the purpose of private study, research, criticism or review, as permitted under the Copyright, Designs and Patents Act, 1988, no part of this publication may be reproduced, stored in a retrieval system, or transmitted in any form or by any means, electronic, electrical, chemical, mechanical, optical, photocopying, recording or otherwise, without the prior written permission of the copyright owner. Enquiries should be addressed to the Publishers.

Every attempt has been made by the Publishers to secure the appropriate permissions for materials reproduced in this book. If there has been any oversight we will be happy to rectify the situation and a written submission should be made to the Publishers.

A CIP catalogue record for this book is available from the British Library.

Shire Library no. 614   •   ISBN-13: 978 0 74780 813 8

Ivan Day has asserted his right under the Copyright, Designs and Patents Act, 1988, to be identified as the author of this book.

Designed by Tony Truscott Designs, Sussex, UK and typeset in Perpetua and Gill Sans.
Printed in China through Worldprint Ltd.

11 12 13 14 15   10 9 8 7 6 5 4 3 2 1

COVER IMAGE
An image from a vintage advertisement for Wall's ice cream.

TITLE PAGE IMAGE
An Italian ice-cream seller, c. 1890.

CONTENTS PAGE IMAGE
A family day at the seaside in the 1950s was not complete without an ice-cream cornet or wafer.

ACKNOWLEDGEMENTS
I would particularly like to thank Anthony Rea for his generosity in sharing his knowledge of the early ice cream families of Manchester and photographs from his collection. I would also like to thank Phil Considine, Robert Hendry, Layinka Swinburne, Robin Weir, Leeanne Westwood, the Guildhall Library and the Wellcome Institute.

Images are acknowledged as follows:
Miss Tina Cox, page 55 (bottom); Daily Mirror Picture Library, pages 51 (bottom) and 53 (bottom); Guildhall Library, City of London, page 9; Robert Hendry, page 14; Tony Muxlow, page 57; Robert Opie Collection, cover, contents page and pages 46 (bottom), 47, 52 (all), 53 (top left and right), and 56; Anthony Rea, pages 40 (bottom), 41 (top and bottom left), 42 (bottom), 43 (top), 46 (top), and 54 (top and bottom); Valence House Museum, London Borough of Dagenham and Barking, page 10; Wellcome Trust, page 11 (top); Robin Weir, page 45 (bottom left).

All other images are from the author's collection.

Shire Publications is supporting the Woodland Trust, the UK's leading woodland conservation charity, by funding the dedication of trees.

CONTENTS

INTRODUCTION

WE ALL have childhood memories of ice cream. Who does not recollect the excitement at hearing the chimes of an ice-cream van, or the heartbreak of one's half-finished lolly sliding off its stick on to a sandy beach? Few, however, will be able to remember the delectable confectioners' ices of the inter-war years, made in smart London establishments such as Gunter's of Berkeley Square, or Jazz Age sundaes with evocative names like Lavender Lady and Aviation Glide, served in nickel-silver cups in Art Deco soda fountains with marble counters, polished chrome taps and ornamental electric light shades. The even more extraordinary ice-cream scene which existed before the First World War has vanished totally into oblivion. A few faded chromolithographs and curious pewter moulds are all that survive of an age when ices were commonly moulded into myriad forms. Artistically crafted ice-cream swans, melons and pineapples nestling in a froth of maidenhair fern and spun sugar were commonplace. Upper-class Victorian diners thought nothing of being served with ices in the shape of castles, elephants or even the Duke of Wellington's boot. Go back still earlier and it is a surprise to learn that there were more flavours on offer in an ice-cream shop in Georgian London than would be found in a twenty-first-century *gelateria*.

When ice cream first appeared in Britain in the seventeenth century, it was a luxury enjoyed solely by the inhabitants of royal palaces and noble households. For two hundred years it remained an upper-class treat. Then, in the middle of the nineteenth century, enterprising Italian vendors started hawking it on the pavements of Victorian cities at a price even street children could afford. During both world wars the Ministry of Food considered ice cream an unnecessary indulgence and its manufacture was outlawed, to conserve precious milk and sugar reserves. When it eventually returned to the British menu, it had been transformed into a factory product mass-marketed by large companies such as Walls and Lyons. Nowadays 600 million litres of ice cream are consumed annually in Britain, an average of roughly 10 litres per person. With annual sales of at least £1.3 billion, ice-cream production is a major element of the British food industry.

Opposite:
Some re-created
Victorian ice
creams. Novelty
moulded ices of
this kind first
appeared in Italy
at the end of the
seventeenth
century.

THE ORIGINS OF ICE CREAM

VARIOUS CHILLED DELICACIES were made by the ancient Chinese, Romans, Persians and others by mixing snow or ice with fruit juice or dairy products. From at least the late medieval period, the Persians and Turks were celebrated for a summer refreshment called *sherbat* or *sherbet*, which was made by whisking ice shavings or snow into sugar syrup and citrus juice. Early English visitors to the Levant were impressed with these snow-cooled beverages and described them with great enthusiasm. In 1615 the Jacobean adventurer and poet George Sandys tells us that they were served in great variety, some even flavoured with perfumes: 'Yet have they sundry sherbets … some made of sugar and lemons, some of violets and the like.' A little later in the century, sherbet powders and concentrates were imported from the Middle East. Just by adding water to these products and chilling them in a cistern of snow or ice, cooling eastern-style sherbets were replicated in London coffee-houses. However, it must be understood that sherbets and their ancient precursors were not true ices. In their most basic form they were really a kind of scented lemonade, sometimes chilled with ice or snow, but never actually frozen.

True ices came about as a result of the discovery of an artificial method of freezing, which harnessed the dramatic refrigerant properties of mixing various chemical salts with crushed ice. Adding saltpetre or common salt to ice decreases the ice's freezing point to well below zero and enables liquids placed in it to be frozen hard rather than just cooled. This phenomenon was first described in Europe in 1530 by an Italian scholar, Marco Zimara. In 1589 the Neapolitan alchemist Giovanni Battista della Porta published some brief instructions for transforming wine into a mouth-chilling slush by means of a mixture of ice and saltpetre. However, it was not until the seventeenth century that these methods were seriously used for freezing food items. In England the technique was described by the natural philosopher Francis Bacon just before he died in 1626, though it is doubtful whether it was actually used in early Stuart kitchens. In high-status households in Italy, a favourite party piece at this time was to freeze fruit or flowers in tall pyramids of crystal-

Opposite:
A sectional plan of an icehouse from Robert Boyle's New Experiments and Observations Touching Cold (London, 1683).

7

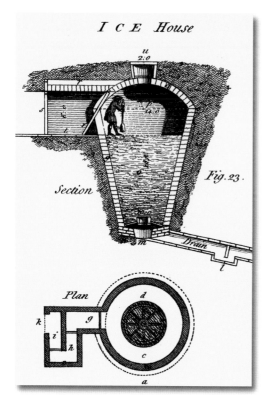

I C E House

Fig. 23.

Section

Plan

A detailed cross-section of an English icehouse showing a worker compacting the ice. The drain is covered by a cartwheel to prevent it becoming blocked by ice.

clear ice as centrepieces for summer banquets. Later in the century very ambitious versions of these glazed table ornaments were created for important state occasions at the Palace of Versailles.

Before artificial freezing could be applied to make any of these frosty novelties, a reliable supply of ice or snow was required – not an easy task in summer. From the medieval period onwards, special underground pits and caves, known as icehouses, were common in parts of Italy and Spain, where compacted snow, gathered during the winter months from nearby mountains, could be stored. The earliest recorded building for ice conservation dates from almost four thousand years ago at Mari in Mesopotamia and is described on a clay tablet in cuneiform script. The ancient Chinese gathered and stored ice as early as 1100 BC for preserving meat and fish. The Greeks and Romans had icehouses too, and compacted snow was on sale in the market in Athens as early as the fifth century.

In England, the earliest icehouses, known at the time as 'snow pits', were built by order of James I in Greenwich in 1619. The principal functions of the ice stored in these structures were for cooling wine and preserving fish and meat. In England the ice was usually collected from frozen ponds and lakes, so icehouses were built close to stretches of water. The resulting ice was dirty and not suitable for putting into drinks, as we do today. When used for cooling wine, the bottles were buried in pulverised ice contained in a cistern. Even later on, when it was used for making ices, the ice and salt mixture never came into contact with the composition being frozen. During the early nineteenth century, much purer ice was shipped from the Arctic. This was cut from the ice floes and was understandably very expensive; an advertisement in _The Times_ in July 1822 read:

> Ice sent to any part of the country. – W. LEFTWICH, 162 Fleet-Street, having imported a cargo of ICE, the Nobility, Gentry, Tavernkeepers, Confectioners, and others, may be supplied with the above article, at 24s. per cwt.

This was the beginning of a major industry. In 1833 a cargo of ice was shipped from Massachusetts to Calcutta. As the nineteenth century progressed, North American and Norwegian ice became a major item of commerce. Icemen delivering blocks of ice by horse and cart were a familiar sight on the streets of Victorian London.

It was in Naples that the technique of artificial freezing seems to have first been applied to freezing oriental-style sherbets, which since at least the early seventeenth century had been known locally as *sorbetti* or *sorbette*. In Florio's Italian/English Dictionary of 1611, the word *sorbetto* is defined as 'a kind of drink used in Turkie made of water and juice of Limonds, Sugar, Amber, and Muske, very costly and delicate'. In 1694 Antonio Latini, a Neapolitan cookery writer, remarked that 'in the city of Naples a great quantity of *sorbette* are consumed, and they are the consistency of sugar and snow, and every Neapolitan, it would seem, is born with the knowledge of how to make them'. Unlike the modern word 'sorbet', which specifically describes a type of water ice, this early Italian usage referred to all types of ices, including those made with milk and cream. In Italy the word *gelato* (from *gelo*, 'ice') did not come into common parlance until the nineteenth century. From Latini's statement it can be assumed that frozen *sorbette* had been available in Naples for several generations. He offers a few basic recipes, including one flavoured with chocolate, but adds that their production was best left to professionals. At this time similar experiments with freezing were being enthusiastically conducted in other Italian cities, in Sicily and in Spain, and a French cookery writer, Audiger, claims to have learnt to make ices in Rome in 1659.

The first printed recipe (for a fruit water ice) was published in France in 1674 by Louis XIV's apothecary, Le Sieur d'Emery. However, his vague instructions result in a hard icy block of frozen strawberry or sour cherry syrup. Much better directions were published in Naples in the 1690s, in an anonymous little booklet entitled *A Brief and New Way to Make with Ease Every Kind of Sorbet*. This work contains twenty-three different recipes, including the earliest for an ice flavoured with vanilla. Among the other varieties are jasmine, candied pumpkin, pinenut, chocolate, pistachio, Portugal orange, Muscat pear, Muscat grape, *torrone* and chestnut. The text also contains the earliest known instructions for making ices into fancy shapes in moulds.

A watercolour of an icehouse in Greenwich Park by Samuel Grimm, 1772. It is possible that this depicts one of the earliest icehouses in Britain, built for James I in 1619.

EARLY ENGLISH ICES

ICE CREAM came to England at a surprisingly early period in its development. It is often claimed that it was first served to Charles I by a French cook called Gérard Tissain, but there is no evidence to support this claim. However, a recipe 'To make Icy Cream' is included in a medical and cookery manuscript, dated 1651–78, by Lady Anne Fanshawe (1625–80), whose husband, Sir Richard, was Charles II's ambassador to Spain. The recipe dates from the mid-1660s, so that her instructions are the earliest in Europe for making a frozen dessert, pre-dating d'Emery's by about a decade. In an acutely observed memoir of her residence in Madrid, she describes how she had watched the king and queen of Spain 'drinking water either cold with snow, or lemonade, or some such thing', but does not mention ice cream as such. It is possible that she learnt the recipe when she was in Spain, but Lady Anne may not have totally understood the process of artificial freezing because the crucial salt or saltpetre required to freeze the mixture is missing from her instructions, so her 'icy cream' would not have frozen. She suggests perfuming 'icy cream' with orange-flower water or ambergris, fashionable ingredients of both Middle Eastern sherbets and other early European ices.

Lady Anne's husband, Sir Richard Fanshawe, was very close to King Charles II. Not only did he attend upon the king at his coronation, but he was sent to Lisbon to accompany Charles's Portuguese bride, Catherine of Braganza, to London. When Charles re-established the Order of the Garter in 1661, Sir Richard attended the great feast held in St George's Hall. No bill of fare survives for this particular dinner, but ten years later ice cream was recorded as an

Lady Anne Fanshawe (1625–80), by Cornelius Johnson, c. 1660. It would appear that Lady Anne was the first European to write down an ice-cream recipe.

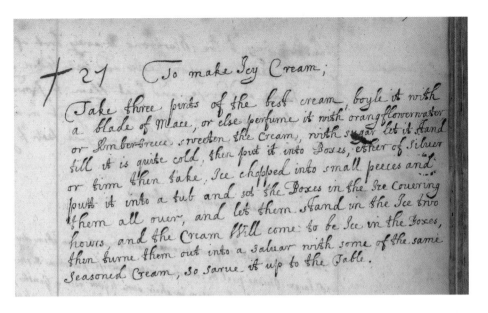

important feature of the banquet course at the 1671 Garter feast. This is the very first record of ice cream on an English menu. However, the frosty treat appeared exclusively on the king's table, where he dined alone. It is likely that Charles II's 'plate of ice cream' was made to a formula like that of Lady Fanshawe's, but there are no records of how it was prepared. Another English recipe for 'ice creame' is recorded in a 1690s manuscript book compiled by Grace, Countess Glanville (1664–1744). Scented with orange-flower water, this glacial delight is almost identical to Lady Anne's 'icy cream', though Lady Glanville's more detailed instructions direct us to freeze the confection in a lidded pan covered with a mixture of ice, alum, salt and saltpetre. From the evidence of these two late-Stuart recipes, it is clear that English ice cream at this period was not agitated as it froze, making it rather hard compared to churned ice creams.

The earliest known recipe for ice cream (c. 1665), from the unpublished manuscript recipe book of Lady Anne Fanshawe, written between 1651 and 1678.

A similar orange-flower ice-cream recipe was published in France in 1692 by the French confectioner Audiger in *La Maison Règle*, an instruction manual explaining how to run a noble

Fully clad for ice cream: Charles II dressed in his Garter robes for a feast at Windsor in 1671.

11

household. Audiger, who was a professional, was the first author to advise that the mixture must be stirred and scraped with a spoon as it freezes, an essential process that prevented large ice crystals from forming, giving the product a smooth texture like that of snow. This crucial technique does not seem to have been understood in England for some time. When Mary Eales, who claimed she was 'Confectioner to her late Majesty Queen Anne', published the first English printed recipe in 1718, she advocated the same *modus operandi* that Lady Fanshawe had described more than sixty years earlier, freezing the mixture solid in tin pots. Even the renowned French chef and confectioner Vincent La Chapelle, who cooked for the fourth Earl of Chesterfield and brought out some very detailed instructions for making both ice creams and water ices in *The Modern Cook* (1733), does not seem to have agitated his mixtures, putting salted ice under and over his freezing vessels for the full duration of the process. However, in a later French issue of his work (1742), he apologises for neglecting to mention in his earlier English editions that the secret of making successful ices was to stir the custard continuously in the freezing pot.

The most interesting aspect of La Chapelle's book is his directions for moulding water ices in the form of realistic fruits. He tells us: 'You must have some leaden Moulds, that have been taken from good Models, and exactly represent the Fruit that you would imitate.' These moulds were sealed

Charles's feast was the earliest recorded occasion at which ice cream was served in Britain. It appeared only on the King's table.

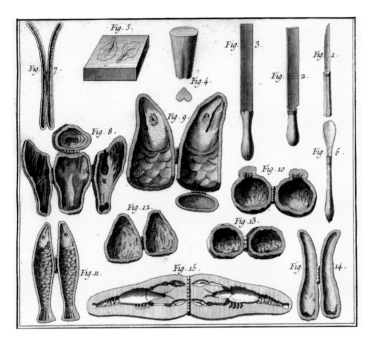

A selection of
ice-cream moulds,
including a carp's
head, a ham,
a crayfish and
a truffle, from
Denis Diderot,
Encyclopédie
(1772).

with a mixture of wax, suet and rosin and plunged into a tub of ice and salt for three hours. The frosty counterfeit fruit were provided with stalks and then painted 'with their natural colour, with Cochineal for the Red, or Saffron or Oker for Yellow. The clever Artist may compose some Mixture of Colours, to imitate more naturally the Colour of the Fruit.' La Chapelle also describes a tin box or pan that could be covered with ice and salt in which the ice fruits, once made, could be prevented from melting. He lists a great variety of fake fruits that could be made in this way, including citrons, oranges, bergamot pears, lemons, peaches, apricots, plums and cherries. By 'leaden', La Chapelle meant not lead but pewter. At this time Thomas Chamberlain, pewterer of King Street in Soho, who started trading in 1732, advertised 'all sorts of Ice Cream & Sugar Moulds' on his trade card. As the craze for these icy novelties grew, more and more English pewterers turned their hand to making the moulds. As with most things relating to ice cream, this fashion was initiated in seventeenth-century Naples. Dr John Moore, an English resident of the city in the late eighteenth century, gives an account of a remarkable dinner served to the King of Naples and his family by the nuns of the convent of San Gregorio Armeno, where the entire meal consisted of counterfeit meat joints, hams, poultry and fish, all artfully moulded from water ices. As will be seen later, joke dishes of this kind spread across Europe and remained fashionable until the First World War.

No 122 @ Burnt Ice Cream. Take 6 eggs. One
gill of syrup. and one pint of Cream: boil it over the fire
untile it becomes thick. then have two ounces of Powd
Sugar in another stew pan and put it over the fire: let
it burn till all melts stirring it all the time & when
you see it is burnt of a fine brown. pour the other in
mix it quickly pass it through a seive & freeze it

No 123. Mill fruit Ice Cream. Take 2 gills
of syrup, squeeze 3 lemons put in a pint of cream
and freeze it cut some lemon peel a little orange
peel and a little angelica, into small peices, when
it is frozen ready to put into the moulds, put
in your Sweetmeats, with a little cochineal: mix
your ingredients well, but not the cochineal as it
must appear only here and there a little red, then
put it into your moulds

No 124. Fresh Currant Ice Cream Take one
pint of currants, pass them through a seive
with 5 oz of Powd Sugar & 1 pint cream then freeze it.

No 125 Burnt Almond Ice Cream. This is done
the same Manner as the filbert ice cream.
No 126. Cedraty Ice Cream, Take 2 large Spoonsful
of essence of cedraty, put it into a bason. squeeze in three
lemons and add one pint of cream. observe that all
the essence is Melted then pass it through a seive &
freeze it. No 127. Parmasan Cheese Ice Cream Take
five eggs. half a pint of syrup & a pint of cream
put them into a stew pan and boil them until it
begins to thicken. then rasp three oz of Parmasan
cheese mix & pass them through a seive & freeze it.

No 128. Damson Ice Cream. Take 3 oz preserved Dam
sons pound them and break the stones of them put them into
a Bason squeeze 2 lemons & a pint of cream press them
through a seive & freeze it.

GEORGIAN FLAVOURS

IT WAS NOT until the middle of the eighteenth century that clear instructions for stirring the ice-cream mixture were published in English. By this time a specialist tool called a 'spaddle' was available, which enabled the ice-cream maker not only to scrape the mixture off the sides of the freezing pot, but also to spin it around, aerating the congealing ice at the same time. Although it seems a very basic technique, making ice cream in this way works extremely well and, when managed properly, can produce a result as good as that made in a modern electric ice-cream maker. Some modern commentators have described the process as difficult and troublesome. They clearly have never had an opportunity to try it out, as it is very easy and freezes the mixture quickly.

During the eighteenth century French confectioners took up the baton from their Italian colleagues and developed ice-cream making in some very creative directions. This was reflected in a number of important publications that appeared in the middle of the century. Among them was the first book devoted entirely to the subject, *L'Art de Bien Faire les Glaces d'Office*, by a confectioner called Emy, published in a single edition in Paris in 1768. This was to be the most influential work on the subject for the next sixty years. Its very large range of recipes and concise instructions show that ices in France had come a long way since d'Emery's primitive frozen syrup. Among Emy's numerous offerings were ices flavoured with rye bread, truffles, rice, *crème de Barbados* liqueur, Tokay wine and burnt sugar.

In France new ways of serving ices were also developed. As early as 1720, faience factories at Rouen and Moustiers were producing specialist three-part ice pails called *seaux à glace*, which were designed to prevent ices from melting when they were served at the table. From 1758 onwards very fine examples of these vessels were made at Sèvres, whose designs were imitated by other European manufactories. English porcelain factories such as Worcester and Spode were quick to bring out their own versions of these attractive vessels, calling them simply 'ice pails'. Josiah Wedgwood, who marketed them under the name 'glaciers', manufactured a variety of designs

Opposite:
A variety of 1780s ice-cream recipes in the handwriting of the London confectioner Frederick Nutt. Flavours include Burnt Ice Cream (caramel), Millefruit, Fresh Currant, Burnt Almond, Parmesan Cheese and Damson. These recipes are reproduced on pages 61–2.

15

A late-eighteenth-
century porcelain
ice pail. There are
three components:
the pail, which is
half-filled with a
mixture of ice and
salt; the liner for
the ice cream; and
a lid, also filled
with salted ice.

in more affordable creamware. These often spectacular vessels went out of use in about 1830, probably as a result of the growing craze for moulded ices.

By the second half of the eighteenth century there were professional confectioners in most cities and major towns in Britain, marketing good-quality ice creams and water ices. Some of these were French, Spanish or Italian émigrés, but there were also plenty of English and Scottish practitioners who had mastered the craft. In 1770 a Mr Borella, 'an ingenius foreigner' who claimed to be the head confectioner to the Spanish ambassador, issued a little book called *The Court and Country Confectioner*, which offered the fullest and clearest instructions to date for freezing ices. His book was aimed not at professionals, but at the huge number of housekeepers and female cooks who wanted to learn the secrets of ice-cream making.

He explains that a pot called a *sorbetiere* was buried in a mixture of ice and salt in a wooden pail. As the mixture freezes, he tells us to

> detach with a pewter spoon, all the flakes which stick to the sides, in order
> to make it congeal equally all over in the pot. Then you must work them
> well as much as you are able, for they are so much the more mellow as they
> are well worked; and their delicacy depends entirely upon that.

D. NEGRI
Confectioner, at the Pine Apple,
in Berkeley Square.
Makes & Sells all Sorts of English, French,
& Italian wet & dryd Sweet Meats.
Cedrati and Bergamot Chips,
Naples Diavolini and Diavoloni
All Sorts of Biskets & Cakes, fine and Common
Sugar Plums, Syrup of Capilaire, Orgeate and
Marsh Mallow, Ghimauve or Lozenges for Colds
& Cough, all Sorts of Ice, Fruits, & Creams, in the
best Italian maner. Likewise furnishes Entertainments in
the newes Fashions, Sells all sorts of Desarts Flowers
Drums & Glass-work at the
lowest Price.

Although Borella's instructions are very clear, his recipes do not give exact proportions for ingredients. He distinguishes between water ices and cream ices and overall offers twenty-four different flavours. These include barberry, tea, white coffee, brown bread, pistachio, pineapple, citron, violet and jasmine, as well as the ubiquitous orange-flower. One of his most interesting offerings is muscadine ice, a lemon and white-currant water ice flavoured with elderflowers, designed to imitate the flavour of muscatel grapes.

Ices were also spreading to the provinces, at least to the dining tables of the owners of great country estates, which were not now considered complete without an icehouse in the grounds. Mary Smith, a housekeeper who had worked for Admiral Lord Anson, the celebrated circumnavigator, at his estate at Shugborough, Staffordshire, and a little later for Sir William Blackett at Wallington Hall in Northumberland, brought out *The Complete Housekeeper* in 1773. In this clearly written and original work, published in

The trade card of Domenico Negri, a confectioner from Turin who sold a variety of Italian ices from his premises in Berkeley Square, London, during the 1760s.

17

A pewter freezing pot and spaddle. This simple but effective apparatus was used to make ice cream from the late seventeenth century until the 1930s.

the fashionable city of Newcastle upon Tyne, there is a good range of excellent ice-cream recipes, some of which are moulded in the form of fruits such as melons, oranges and citrons. Most interesting, though, are her directions for moulding a raspberry ice cream in a fluted mould, the first reference to a 'pillar ice', an ornamental ice that would become very popular in the following century.

One of Borella's contemporaries in London was Domenico Negri, an important Italian confectioner who opened a shop in Berkeley Square, at the Sign of the Pineapple, in 1759. Negri, who was from Turin, eventually went into partnership with an English confectioner, James Gunter, and changed the name of the premises to the 'Pot and Pineapple'. Sited in fashionable Mayfair, the Berkeley Square premises became the most prestigious outlet for ices in Georgian London and was patronised by the Prince of Wales and his brothers. Negri's delicious ice creams and water ices were legendary. Though he never committed any of his recipes to paper, two of his apprentices went on to write books on confectionery, with chapters on ices even more extensive than Borella's. The first of these, *The Housekeeper's Valuable Present* (*c.* 1780s), by Robert Abbot, included a good range of flavours, though there was nothing completely original among them.

However, a more important work by Frederick Nutt, 'Late an Apprentice to the well-known Messrs. Negri and Witten, of Berkley Square', called *The Complete Confectioner*, was brought out in 1789. This work was a milestone in the history of ice cream in Britain, because its recipes were the first to contain clear instructions and exact measurements. Nutt also advocated making his ices with syrup rather than powdered sugar. The evidence of Nutt's recipes indicated that he clearly understood that the ratio of sugar to liquid was critical in making a high-quality product: too much sugar and it would not freeze properly; too little and it would be rough with ice crystals. The thirty-one recipes for ice creams and the twenty-four for water ices may have been learnt from his master, Domenico Negri. There are certainly some that are very similar to ices made in Italy at this time. Nutt's Royal Ice Cream, rich in egg yolks and flavoured with orange-flower water, preserved peel and

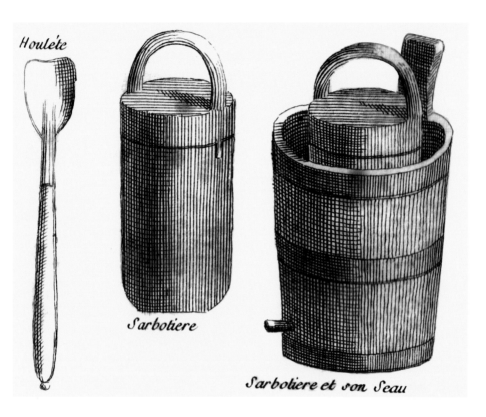

Houléte

Sarbotiere

Sarbotiere et son Seau

pistachio nuts, is identical to a recipe called *Sorbetto di Napoli alla Mirolig*, published in Negri's home city of Turin in 1790. The book in which this appeared, *Il Confetturiere Piemontese*, the most up-to-date Italian work on the subject at the time, contains only twenty-five recipes for ices compared to Nutt's total of fifty-five. Some of Nutt's more unusual flavours include burnt filbert, ginger, bergamot, Seville orange and Parmesan cheese. The last was based on a French recipe, rather than an Italian one. In its original 1751 French form, the Parmesan ice cream was moulded into the shape of a wedge of cheese, with a rind simulated in caramelised sugar. This unexpectedly delicious concoction remained popular in England for over fifty years. Nutt's punch water ice was a frozen version of the ardent rum punch that had been a favourite English vice since the late seventeenth century. It was eventually transformed by some unknown Italian confectioner into *punch à la romaine*, a frothy confection of maraschino, meringue, lemon water ice and champagne, which became the favoured refreshment at ball suppers and other patrician entertainments for the best part of a century.

Woodcut of ice cream equipment from Emy, *L'Art de Bien Faire Les Glaces D'Office* (Paris: 1768). *Houléte* is the French name for the ice cream spaddle.

BOMBES AND ICE PUDDINGS

JAMES GUNTER, Negri's former partner, founded a dynasty of London ice-cream makers who continued to trade until the 1930s. Gunter's was an aristocratic establishment and its ices were not cheap. After a mild winter, when ice was difficult to procure, prices rose even further. In July 1822 the following advertisement was placed in *The Times*:

> Messrs Gunter respectfully beg to inform the nobility and those who honour them with their commands, that having this day received one of their cargoes of ice by the *Platoff*, from the Greenland Seas, they are enabled to supply their CREAM and FRUIT ICES at their former prices. 7 Berkeley Square.

One of Gunter's employees was a talented young Italian confectioner from Colorno near Parma, Giuliagmo Jarrin, who in 1820 published *The Italian Confectioner*, with a large chapter on ice creams and water ices. Jarrin was a master of his craft, celebrated for his intricate sugar table sculpture and ornamental Twelfth Night cakes. His book is the first in English to include illustrations of the equipment used to make ice cream. He describes the process clearly: 'keep turning the pots quickly round about in the ice, by means of the handle at [the] top, till the cream is set, opening them every three minutes, and with a copper spaddle take the contents from the edges, mixing and stirring the whole well together.' His recipes include alcoholic flavours such as champagne water ice and maraschino ice cream. Maraschino, a clear spirit distilled from sour cherries, was starting to take over from orange-flower water as the most fashionable ice-cream flavouring at this period. Although a recipe for *glace de marasquin* was published by Emy in France in 1768, Jarrin was the first to describe its use in England. It remained the flavouring of choice for the high-class ice-cream maker until the early twentieth century. One of Jarrin's most interesting recipes is for a *bomba* ice, the first use of this term to describe any member of the ice-cream family. It was a richly aerated mousse of cream and egg yolks, rather like a frozen *zabaglione*, but was left in the freezing pot to become solid and turned out to

Opposite:
A nineteenth-century ice cream in the form of a flower basket with a selection of garnishing ices.

21

Giuliagmo Jarrin, another London-based Italian, who included a comprehensive chapter on ices in his influential book The Italian Confectioner (London, 1820).

resemble an artillery shell – hence the name, which means 'bomb'. It started a long-lasting craze for bomb-shaped ices, some of them even made in the form of an anarchist's round bomb complete with spun-sugar flames issuing from the fuse. In winter, when fresh fruit was not available, it had been common practice to use preserved fruit jellies and jams to make ices. Jarrin was the first in England to advocate the use of bottled fruit, a process recently invented by his contemporary Nicholas Appert.

Although Gunter and other high-class confectioners dominated professional production, there was a growing interest in small-scale domestic ice-cream making, at least in the kitchens of the wealthy. Inventories of equipment in nineteenth-century kitchens frequently include ice-cream moulds and other icing equipment. Some of the more palatial establishments even had cool rooms equipped with ice-storage chests and a good supply of freezing pots, spaddles and ice-cream moulds to cater for very ambitious entertainments. In 1832 the architect Jeffry Wyatville designed the sixth Duke of Devonshire's new kitchen complex at Chatsworth House in Derbyshire, and among the warren of basement rooms that formed the kitchen offices he constructed a cold room with a large built-in chest for storing ice from the two icehouses in the grounds. Many items of kitchen

These copper bombe moulds have a screw to allow the air in for an easy release. One has a special lid which creates a cavity that can be filled with another flavour to create a bombe surprise.

French pewter ice-cream moulds from a catalogue of Cadot of Paris, 1890s. Large numbers of moulds made by French firms were shipped into Britain during the nineteenth century. Note the ice-cream anarchist's 'bomb'.

equipment from this period have survived at Chatsworth, including a large variety of ice-cream moulds and other ice-making utensils.

As the Industrial Revolution progressed, more specialised equipment was manufactured, and a bewildering number of pewter, copper and tin ice moulds were launched. Many of the popular cookery books of the Victorian period give directions for making ices, and some have extensive recipe sections. A highly refined Anglo-French style of cuisine was fashionable

Pewter moulds from the catalogue of Biertumpfel & Son of Regent's Park, London, founded in 1831.

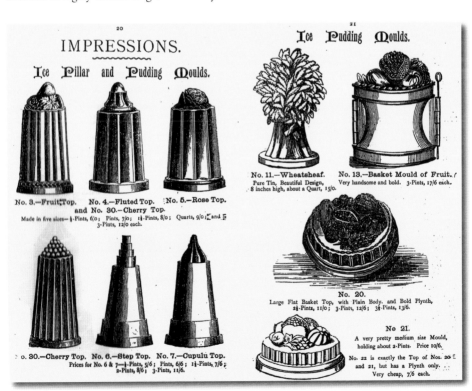

20

IMPRESSIONS.

Ice Pillar and Pudding Moulds.

No. 3.—Fruit Top.   No. 4.—Fluted Top.   No. 5.—Rose Top.
and No. 30.—Cherry Top.
Made in five sizes—½-Pints, 6/0 ;   Pints, 7/0 ;   1½-Pints, 8/0 ;   Quarts, 9/0 ;   and
3-Pints, 12/0 each.

: o. 30.—Cherry Top.   No. 6.—Step Top.   No. 7.—Cupula Top.
Prices for No. 6 & 7—½-Pints, 5/6 ;   Pints, 6/6 ;   1½-Pints, 7/6 ;
2-Pints, 8/6 ;   3-Pints, 11/6.

21

Ice Pudding Moulds.

No. 11.—Wheatsheaf.
Pure Tin, Beautiful Design,
8 inches high, about a Quart, 15/0.

No. 13.—Basket Mould of Fruit.
Very handsome and bold.   3-Pints, 17/6 each.

No. 20.
Large Flat Basket Top, with Plain Body, and Bold Plynth,
2½-Pints, 11/0 ;   3-Pints, 12/6 ;   3½-Pints, 13/6.

No 21.
A very pretty medium size Mould,
holding about 2-Pints.   Price 10/6.

No. 22 is exactly the Top of Nos. 20
and 21, but has a Plynth only.
Very cheap, 7/6 each.

23

A Victoria Ice Pudding. The chef Charles Elmé Francatelli designed this intricate ice-cream centrepiece to honour his employer, Queen Victoria.

among the Victorian upper classes, so many of the ices of the period were given smart French names, even when they were invented by English confectioners. Some of these creations demanded great skill by the practitioner and it must be remembered that all were created without the benefit of freezers or electricity.

One of Queen Victoria's chefs, Charles Elmé Francatelli, was noted for the complexity of his ice-cream centrepieces. One, which he named 'Iced Pudding à la Victoria' in honour of the queen, consisted of a realistic melon moulded out of almond-flavoured ice cream, crowned and surrounded with smaller moulded ices in the form of miniature pineapples and apricots. The surface of the melon was encrusted with chopped pistachios and almonds to imitate the rugged skin of a real melon, and the whole arrangement was placed on a stand in the form of entwined dolphins moulded in ice and hung with sugar-paste bladder wrack. Francatelli also offered detailed instructions for making a realistic boar's head out of sponge cake filled with ice cream in two colours, 'in imitation of flesh – pink and white – to give it the appearance of fat and lean in natural layers'. This was a continuation of that old joke of making realistic joints of meat out of ice cream. Similar *trompe l'oeil* iced puddings were made in the form of hams, one remarkable example being surrounded with ice-cream champagne bottles and corks. Perhaps the most popular of these novelties was a bundle of individually moulded ice-cream asparagus spears, usually tied up with silk ribbons. Francatelli can also be credited as the first chef to serve ice cream in wafer cones. His Iced Pudding à la Chesterfield of 1846, a frozen pudding moulded in the form of a pyramid, was surrounded with little wafer cornucopias filled with pineapple ice cream. Complex confections featuring wafer cones packed with ice cream became increasingly popular on the tables of the rich, but it was not until the early years of the twentieth century that they were used for serving cheap ices on the streets.

One of the most popular frozen desserts of the nineteenth century was Nesselrode Pudding, a moulded chestnut ice cream, enriched with succulent dried fruit and maraschino liqueur. It was probably invented by Monie, *chef de cuisine* to the Russian diplomat Karl Vasilyevich Nesselrode. Monie's intention was to poke fun at English food, as his original Nesselrode Pudding was moulded in a pig's bladder to make it resemble a rotund plum pudding.

Ice puddings from Francatelli's The Modern Cook (London, 1846). The Chesterfield Pudding on the right is garnished with ice-cream cornets filled with pineapple ice. This is the earliest English record of ice cream served in cones.

Ice cream was also spreading down the social scale. By the end of the Victorian period, these complicated dishes were no longer confined to the tables of aristocrats. Writing in 1902, the cookery author S. Beaty-Powell tells us:

Joke ice creams in the form of cuts of meat had been popular since the middle of the eighteenth century. This Victorian extravaganza also includes ice-cream champagne bottles and corks.

> Not so many years ago an ice pudding was looked upon as a triumph of culinary art, that even the average good professed cook would as soon have thought of trying to make, as of trying to fly; whilst the ordinary ices, served on plates at ball suppers &c., came as a matter of course from the confectioner's. Now, however, thanks to various improvements in freezers, ice caves, &c., ice-making has become less of a secret, and very few really good cooks would confess to be ignorant of its preparation; whilst almost every house-mistress intent on a smart dinner would insist on an iced *entremet* of some kind.

Thomas Masters's ice-cream machine, patented in 1843. Masters's invention was the first hand-churned machine to appear in England. Nancy Johnson, a Philadelphia housewife, patented a similar machine in the United States in the same year.

William Fuller patented this ice-cream machine in 1856. It was more primitive than Masters's device, requiring the operator to scrape the congealing ice from the rotating drum with a spaddle.

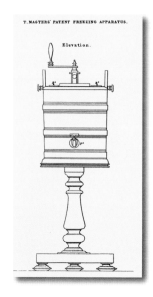

T. MASTERS' PATENT FREEZING APPARATUS.

Elevation.

During the 1840s and 1850s a number of hand-cranked ice-cream freezers appeared on the market. Although they had simple mechanised features, they still used a mixture of ice and salt as a refrigerant. In 1843 Thomas Masters, author of a major work on ice and ice cream, *The Ice Book* (London, 1844), patented a machine which he claimed could not only make ice cream, but also manufacture clean clear ice and be used to churn butter and cool wine. A more basic device, patented by William Fuller in 1856, rotated a large drum-like pot in a wooden ice pail, the operator having to scrape the congealing ice from its sides in the old-fashioned way with a spaddle. Both Masters and Fuller claimed these new utensils were easier to use than the usual freezing pot and enabled more air to be churned into the mixture, resulting in a lighter product. However, many professionals continued to use freezing pots until the 1920s.

Both Masters and Fuller published collections of ice-cream recipes. One of Masters's most interesting ices was Howqua's Tea Ice Cream, flavoured with a popular blend of tea named after the wealthy Cantonese merchant Wu Bingjian (1769–1843), known in the West at this time as Howqua. Other than this, his collection contains nothing new. On the other hand, Fuller's numerous recipes for Neapolitan-style ices are rich in interesting and novel flavours, as well as new techniques. It is possible that he obtained some of his recipes from Italian confectioners resident in London at the time. His formula for basic ice-cream custard was fluffed up with meringue, a refinement which made for a lighter type of ice, known later in the century as a *parfait* or *spongada*. His numerous recipes include such delicacies as Iced Polenta Pudding, Iced Apple Pudding and the evocatively named Love Ice, as well as intriguing water ices in such flavours as cucumber and China root. The latter was perfumed with *Smilax china*, an oriental rhizome with a flavour like sarsaparilla.

As the nineteenth century progressed, many new forms of ices appeared on upper-class tables. The Moscovite was a lightly frozen ice-cream pudding thickened with gelatine or isinglass. It had the advantage of not requiring a freezing pot or ice-cream machine. A sealed mould full of the prepared mixture needed just to be plunged into a pail of ice and salt until the mixture was firm, but not solidly frozen. However, it was easier to freeze this kind of ice in a small cupboard or metal cylinder like that described by La Chapelle in 1733. These so-called 'ice caves' usually had hollow walls that could be charged with a mixture of ice and salt. They proved to be an effective way of freezing iced mousses and related dishes. One of the most popular ices of this kind was the frozen biscuit, really a kind of mousse. Recipes varied, but many frequently did contain pulverised biscuit crumbs. They were frozen in small fancy paper cases and became very popular towards the end of the century. Manufacturers of culinary paper requisites vied with each other to produce new designs for ice-biscuit cases, their forms becoming ever fussier.

Based on an American design, this type of churn freezer was popular before the First World War for domestic use. Professionals used much larger models, which were usually turned by mechanical means.

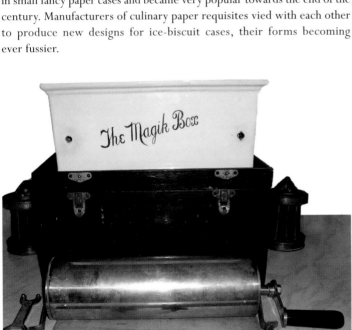

This unusual ice-cream machine from the 1920s worked in the opposite way to most other models. Salt and ice were put in the metal drum, which was rotated in a ceramic bath filled with the mixture to be frozen.

Fancy paper cases were very popular at the end of the nineteenth century for serving biscuits glacés and other small ices.

FANCY ICE AND SOUFFLET CASES.

Arum Lily Basket.

The Girdle Basket.

Daffodil.

	Per doz.
Girdle Ice Case, pink, ruby, apple green, or amber	1/9
Sunbonnet Ice Case, pink, yellow, or green	2/6
Snowdrop Basket, yellow or green ...	3/3
Daffodil Basket, yellow or green	3/3
Girdle Basket, red, pink, green or amber	3/9
Orchid Basket, yellow, green, or pink	5 0

		Per doz.
Arum Lily Basket, yellow, green or pink	...	4 0
Canterbury Bell Ice Case, white, pink or blue		3 0
Daffodil Ice Case, yellow		3/3
Eucharis Ice Case, white or pink	...	3 0
Shell Ice Case, pink or green	...	2 9
Orange Blossom Ice Case	...	each 10d.

The Turkey Ice Case, 9d. each; 8/9 per doz.

Towards the end of the nineteenth century ices began to enjoy considerable social esteem among the burgeoning professional classes – even a dinner party in a well-appointed suburban villa was not complete without a fancy ice of some kind gracing the entremets course or dessert. Many London hostesses bought them in from confectioners' shops and from large establishments, such as the Army and Navy Stores, where a 10-shilling

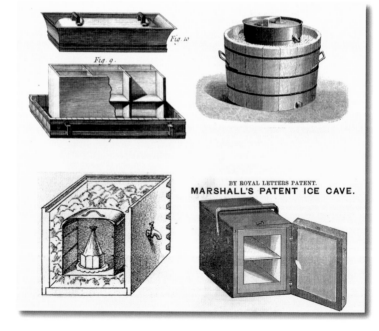

Fig. 10

Fig. 9.

BY ROYAL LETTERS PATENT.
MARSHALL'S PATENT ICE CAVE.

So-called 'ice caves' were early types of freezer, first described in 1733. The inner containers were surrounded by a mixture of ice and salt, enabling a moulded ice placed inside to be frozen hard and conserved for hours.

deposit was charged on the ice pail and bucket required for conveying the frozen delicacy home. However, a growing number of domestic servants were becoming capable of making them in their own employers' kitchens. Cooks and housekeepers, ignorant of the equipment and techniques required, were sent by their mistresses to ice-cream-making lessons at privately run cookery schools. The most important of these was the Mortimer Street School of Cookery in London, founded by Felix and Mary Anne Lavenue in 1857. In 1885 the premises were taken over by an entrepreneurial genius, Agnes B. Marshall, who not only wrote two best-selling books on ice-cream making, but also retailed a comprehensive range of ice-making equipment and moulds.

Among Marshall's stock were a number of her own inventions, including a highly successful patent ice-cream machine, which she marketed in a range

A variety of novelty ices from Theodore Garrett's, The Encyclopaedia of Practical Cookery (London, 1890s).

MOULDS FOR THESE DESIGNS CAN BE HAD OF A.B. MARSHALL.

Striking moulded ices like these published by Agnes Marshall were very fashionable during the closing decades of the nineteenth century.

of sizes. Marshall claimed that the rapidity of freezing with this apparatus was such that 'smooth and delicious ice can be produced in three minutes'. She also retailed a range of patent ice caves, which could be utilised not only 'for setting ice pudding and freezing soufflés', but 'for keeping ices during Ball, Evening and Garden Parties, and for taking ice creams &c., to Races, Picnics &c'. Marshall was also the first to advocate the use of liquid gas to make ice cream.

Marshall's *The Book of Ices* (1885) contains an extensive range of basic recipes for ice creams, water ices, sorbets, bombes and ice puddings and is illustrated with a range of striking chromolithographs of frozen desserts. In 1894 she issued *Fancy Ices*, a collection of much more ambitious frozen dishes, most of them dependent on the kind of specialised moulds sold in the shop below her cookery school. Many of these were decorated with frothy fronds of maidenhair fern and surrounded by smaller garnishing ices. Some were highly exotic. Sultan Pudding was a cream ice flavoured with vanilla, maraschino and Turkish delight, and moulded in the shape of a mosque. It was surrounded with a compote of sultanas and diced Turkish delight. Her Rosseline Bombe was a sugarloaf-shaped cone of rum and rosewater ice cream sheathed in a dome of spun sugar dappled with crystallised cherries. As well as her large centrepieces, there were small individual ices in the form of miniature fruits placed in cups made of frozen water or miniature baskets of nougat. Single serving ices like these were ideally suited to ambitious entertainments such as ball suppers. The author tells us more:

Agnes Marshall's patent freezer first appeared in the 1880s. Its inventor claimed it could freeze a pint of ice cream in three minutes.

At large parties two sorts of ices are usually served, and should be carefully contrasted. A pleasing variety is often produced by filling little moulds with different kinds of ice, which are then served in tiny lace paper cups, under the name of *glaces assorties*, or else the different colours and flavours are placed in the same mould either regularly or not; in the latter case they produce a marbled effect, suggestive of the Venetian glass known as *millefiori or colorito*.
Another very popular form is the Neapolitan ice, or *crème panachée* as it is sometimes called, which is produced by filling a metal box, made for the purpose, with layers of differently flavoured and coloured cream and water ices; for instance, lemon, vanilla, chocolate, and pistachio. When moulded, these are turned out, cut across in slices, and, served in little paper lace cases, offer the requisite variety to both sight and palate.

This steel engraving from Agnes Marshall's Fancy Ices (London, 1894) represents a frozen dessert called a Catherine Basket. It is surrounded by smaller garnishing ices and decorated with fronds of maidenhair fern.

Agnes Marshall's readership consisted of well-off housewives, housekeepers and professional cooks who were interested in making ices at home. The professional confectioners, pastrycooks and caterers who made ices for their livelihood were more reserved about publishing their secrets. However, towards the end of the century, a baker and pastrycook called Frederick Vine brought out two little books aimed at the trade that give a rare insight into the world of the commercial high-class ice-cream maker in the late Victorian period. One of these books, *Ices: Plain and Decorated* (1899), contains many basic recipes but also gives detailed directions for making very advanced frozen centrepieces, known as iced trophies. These were even more ambitious

A modern re-creation of Mrs Marshall's Catherine Basket.

A catalogue
illustration of the
mould used to
make the ice
cream illustrated
at the beginning of
this chapter, 1880s.

The two-part
pewter mould
used to make the
basket of flowers,
c. 1880.

than Mrs Marshall's spectacular creations. Vine's patriotic Iced Trophy *à la Britannique* required at least four moulds, one in the form of the figure of Britannia, the others in the shape of a seated lion, a small ship, and also a large round bombe mould. The last was used to make a globe of green grape ice, complete with continents and oceans. The ship's hull, moulded from rose-flavoured ice with a vanilla-ice deck, had rigging constructed from pulled caramel, and sails of rice paper. Britannia herself was formed out of redcurrant water ice and furnished with a caramel trident. The lion was moulded from chocolate ice cream, its eyes and mane gilded with gold leaf. This complex and impressive dish was put together from custards and water ices frozen in the time-honoured way,

Neapolitan cups, from Agnes B. Marshall, *Fancy Ices* (London, 1894). These little ice cups are filled with ice creams in the form of roses garnished with maidenhair fern.

the moulded ices being plunged into tubs of ice and salt, and the whole ensemble prevented from melting by keeping it in an ice cave. A skilled chef today would struggle to create such a demanding *tour de force*, even with the benefit of electrical freezers and other modern technology.

Some of the moulds used to make the garnishing ices: a raspberry tart, a lemon, a potato and a crown on a cushion.

Two pewter
moulds: one
to make the
ice-cream rose
(upper) and one
to make the ice
cup (lower).

Neapolitan
cups re-created.
Cups and goblets
moulded out of
ice were popular
at the end of the
Victorian period
for individual
servings of ice
cream and sorbet.

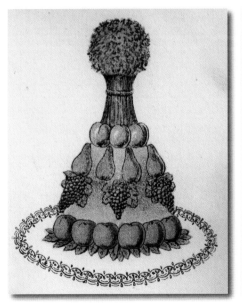

Top Left: Frederick Vine's Iced Trophy à la
Britannique, a chromolithograph illustration
from his Ices Plain and Decorated (London, 1899).

Top right and bottom two: A selection of ice
puddings and compotes (cold cooked fruit
enclosed in ice-cream containers), also from Vine.

35

ICES FOR ALL

B Y THE middle of the nineteenth century cheap ices were being sold on the streets of London by pedlars. Ice cream was so much associated with upper-class life that many doubted it would appeal to ordinary folk. One street trader, interviewed by Henry Mayhew in 1851, was very sceptical: 'Ices in the streets! Aye and there'll be jellies next, and then mock turtle, and then the real ticket, sir … Penny glasses of champagne, I shouldn't wonder.' Mayhew reported that ices were first sold in the open air in the summer of 1850 by a speculator, who organised a gang of street pedlars. He bought his ice cream from a Holborn confectioner and sold it on to the hawkers, but found it an unprofitable business and eventually emigrated to the United States. Mayhew reports that soon after this another trader, who owned one of Masters's patent freezers, started selling home-made ices in Petticoat Lane, but his business was also short-lived.

It seems that English working-class people found eating such cold food an uncomfortable experience. Another street seller interviewed by Mayhew explained:

> Yes, Sir, I mind very well the first time I ever sold ices. I don't think they'll ever take greatly in the streets. But there is no saying. Lord! How I have seen the people splutter when they've tasted them for the first time … One young Irish fellow – he bought an ice of me, and when he had scraped it all together with the spoon, he made a pull at it as if he was drinking beer. In course it was all among his teeth in less than no time, and he stood like a stattey for an instant, and then roared out, – 'Jasus! I am kilt. The coald shivers is on to me.'

The same trader told Mayhew that his best customers were servant maids: 'Pr'aps they'd been used, some on 'em, to get a taste of ices on the sly before, in their services.' When Mayhew's great chronicle of London working-class life, *London Labour and the London Poor*, came out in 1851, he reported that there were only twenty street vendors purveying ice cream in the capital,

Opposite:
By the middle of the nineteenth century ices were no longer just for the wealthy and were becoming available even to poor street children.

37

A crowd on Hampstead Heath during a heatwave in 1881 enjoying penny and twopenny ices from a busy Italian vendor.

compared to three hundred hawking cooked sheep's trotters and 150 selling pickled whelks. He calculated that the whole trade in street ice cream in the city was worth only £42, amounting to a total annual sale of ten thousand penny ices.

Despite this slow start, there was a dramatic increase in street hawkers selling cheap ice cream as a result of an influx of immigrants from Italy in the second half of the nineteenth century. Political upheavals and economic stagnation at home forced many rural Italians to seek a better life in Britain. Earlier in the century, skilled Italian gold workers, instrument makers and gilders had been attracted to the Hatton Garden area of London, where a few educated political refugees had already formed a small expatriate colony in the eighteenth century. By the 1860s the community was augmented by waves of less skilled economic migrants from impoverished rural areas, some of whom sought a precarious living on the streets as itinerant musicians, organ grinders or chestnut sellers. During the warm summer months many would venture on to the streets with handcarts and sell ices, usually under the control of English-speaking *padroni*. They were more persistent in their enterprises than Mayhew's English pedlars and by the 1860s Italian ice-cream men were a familiar sight throughout the capital.

In Saffron Hill and Eyre Street Hill, Holborn, there were many cheap, overcrowded lodging houses where the poorer settlers made their first London homes. It was in the cool cellars of these buildings that the ices sold on the streets were made. In the early days there seems to have been a great deal of exploitation of newly arrived immigrants by unscrupulous bosses. Wages were low, and accommodation squalid and overcrowded. The Italians were also often badly treated by local gangs of English hooligans, who would sometimes throw dirty material into their ice-cream pots.

This sketch by Paul Renouard entitled 'Whitechapel Way – Unseasonable Refreshment – A November Scene in the East End' appeared in the Graphic in December 1891.

As well as immigrants from Italy proper, many from Ticino, the Italian-speaking canton of Switzerland, settled in the neighbourhood. Among their ranks were *chocolatiers* and confectioners who started more respectable and well-appointed shops. The most successful of these was Carlo Gatti (1817–78), who arrived in London in 1847. He started by selling wafers and chestnuts from a handcart in the Holborn area, but by 1851 he had founded a smart shop on the corner of Leather Lane and High Holborn, and a café-restaurant in Hungerford Market which sold ices and pastries. He seems to have been the first wholesale ice-cream maker in England, claiming in 1858 that he was selling ten thousand penny ices in a single day. Eventually he made a very

Office boys and messengers were often tempted by a quick penny lick while out on their errands. Postcard, c. 1911.

Nineteenth-century émigré ice-cream vendors frequently wore their regional Italian costume. Note the strategic location of this handcart near a toy shop.

An Italian ice-cream workshop with pewter freezing pots and a large mechanical churn. From Enrico Grifoni, Trattato di Gelateria (Milan, 1911).

A rare view of an early ice-cream dairy, very similar to that in the previous illustration, in Manchester, c. 1890s. Note the large freezing pails and huge spaddle.

large fortune importing ice from Norway. One of Gatti's ice caves on the Regent's Canal still survives.

Other Italians sought their fortunes in the north of England, Scotland and Wales. Manchester attracted many skilled terrazzo workers, plasterers and stonemasons, who found work on the new town hall under construction from 1868 to 1877. They settled in the Ancoats district of the city, which, like the Clerkenwell Road area in Holborn, became known as Little Italy. Many of these hard-working and enterprising folk, once they had established themselves, sponsored young men from their own villages to come and work for them, and so the community grew. By the 1880s a number of families had founded ice-cream businesses and were selling their wares from handcarts around the city. These close-knit families proved to have considerable commercial acumen and their businesses frequently lasted for three or four generations, with a number still trading today.

One Ancoats pioneer, and the founder of an ice-cream dynasty,

Horse-drawn carts became increasingly popular with street vendors. This one was owned by the Burgon (formerly Boggiano) family of Salford.

was Carmine 'Carlo' Tiani from the Valle di Comino in Lazio. He came to Manchester in the 1880s and rapidly established himself as a successful retailer, importing Italian foodstuffs and manufacturing ices and wafers in the cellar beneath his shop. Carlo's Ices, as his business came to be known, was one of the first in Manchester to use mechanised freezers. The increased production enabled Carlo to expand his trade and he eventually had seven pony carts and three handcarts purveying ices in the streets of Hulme and Moss Side. Carlo's daughter Brigida married another Lazio native, the

Below left: Antonio Arcaro, one of the early Italian ice-cream vendors on the streets of Manchester, c. 1900.

Below right: A large commercial ice pail and freezing pot with brass handle (1890s). The pot is of the kind used on handcarts and holds 3 gallons of ice cream.

Ice-cream carts were still popular in the 1920s, when this advertisement was published, but were eventually superseded by tricycles, motorcycle combinations and vans.

W·GOODYEAR&SONS LTD
Industrial Truck Works, DUDLEY, Worcs.

A few designs of our well known
**ICE CREAM
· CARTS ·**

Also Makers of
INDUSTRIAL TRUCKS and TROLLEYS for all trades
AND THE
GOODYEAR GREENBAT 2 TON ELECTRIC TRUCK
AS USED BY THE
LEADING MANUFACTURERS, DOCK and RAILWAY COMPANIES.

Both hand and horse-drawn carts were often lavishly decorated. This attractive example belonged to the Granelli family, whose dairy was in the Oldham Road in Manchester.

entrepreneurial Vincenzo Schiavi, who, from humble beginnings as a street seller with one cart in 1900, expanded his business to become a major Manchester ice-cream trader, known to all in the city as Vincent's Ices. With the help of his wife's business skills and experience in food retailing, he opened an ice-cream factory and in the 1920s upgraded from horse-drawn carts to motorised vehicles. His catchphrase, 'Vinnie's ices – good for the ladies, makes bonny babies', is still remembered in Salford.

The Reas, another branch of this enterprising family, are still trading today. Their business was founded by Marco Rea, from the Frosinone area of Lazio. Marco,

Three generations
of a Manchester
ice cream family:
left, Carmine
'Carlo' Tiani;
centre, Vincenzo
Schiavi; right,
Marco Rea.

who was born in 1889, worked initially as a travelling entertainer at fairs but eventually settled into the ice-cream business. Like many Italian men, Marco was interned during the Second World War, but he re-established his business in the late 1940s, modernising his plant and setting up a fleet of smart ice-cream vans. The story of this Italian family is similar to that of hundreds of others who settled in Britain, founded successful businesses and became valued and respected members of the community.

In the early days there was considerable prejudice against Italian ice-cream vendors, particularly from the established English confectioners. In 1901 Frederick Vine was worried about the competition and recommended that more of his colleagues should sell ices so that they could 'put into their pockets what too often goes into that of the swarthy sons of Italy, who annually visit us with their gaudily-painted barrows and questionable ices'. Beaty-Powell was also jingoistic, comparing 'the delicate variety obtainable at the first-rate confectioners, to the awful "hokey-pokey" of the Italian ice-cream vendor at street corners, the delight of the street Arab, and the horror of the microbe and bacillus hunter'.

'Hokey-pokey' was a generic name for any kind of cheap ice cream sold and consumed on the street. The term may have been derived from the Italian street cry '*O' che poco!*' ('Oh how little!'), meaning how little it cost – usually a penny, but the true origin can only be guessed at. 'Hokey-pokey' also referred to a specific kind of ice sold by the hawkers, who became universally known as 'hokey-pokey men' or 'ice jacks'. This was a small slice cut from a brick of multi-coloured ice cream and was more or less identical to Mrs Marshall's

How to make hokey-pokey, the Victorian precursor of the 'brick'. The final product was wrapped in waxed paper and stored on the handcart in a freezing pot. From Frederick Vine, Ices for Shop Sale (London, 1899).

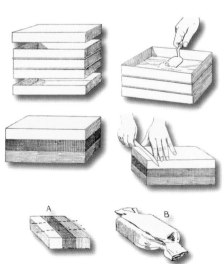

Hokey-pokey was a poor relative of the Neapolitan ice or crème panachée, favoured by rich Victorians. No doubt children found its colours attractive, but its ingredients were often cheap and nasty.

The illustration below shows the traditional method of filling a penny lick. To the right of this are three examples of the glasses, made out of pressed glass in many forms. Their thick shallow bowl created an illusion that convinced the customer that he was getting a generous serving.

fashionable Neapolitan ice, or *crème panachée*, but made from much cheaper ingredients. The Victorian author Andrew Tuer, in his book *Old London Street Cries* (1885), tells us more:

> Parti-coloured Neapolitan ices, vended by unmistakable natives of Whitechapel or the New Cut, whose curious cry of "Okey Pokey' originated no one knows how, have lately appeared in the streets. Hokey Pokey is of a firmer make and probably stiffer material than the penny ice of the Italians, which it rivals in public favour; and it is built up of variously flavoured layers. Sold in halfpenny and also penny paper-covered squares, kept until wanted in a circular metal refrigerating pot surrounded by broken ice, Hokey Pokey has the advantage over its rival eaten from glasses, inasmuch as it can be carried away by the purchaser and consumed at leisure. Besides being variously flavoured, Hokey Pokey is dreadfully sweet, dreadfully cold, and hard as a brick. It is whispered that the not

unwholesome Swede turnip, crushed into pulp, has been known to form its base, in lieu of more expensive supplies from the cow, whose complex elaboration of cream from turnips is thus unceremoniously abridged.

A far cry from the elaborate full-cream ices of the wealthy, the recipe used by most street sellers was a mixture of water, cornflour and sugar. Note the brass-handled freezing pot, typical of those used on handcarts.

The inclusion of turnips in the composition was a popular myth. One of the few surviving recipesdemonstrates that hokey-pokey was actually made from a mixture of cornflour, water, gelatine, sugar, flavourings and colour.

Below left: A hygiene scare in 1901 resulted in a rash of xenophobic postcards. The Italian street vendor is serving one customer with a penny lick, while the boy in the foreground has carelessly discarded his paper hokey-pokey wraps.

The glasses mentioned by Tuer were the famous penny licks, which every street vendor used to serve his ices. They were of thick pressed glass and were made in three sizes: halfpenny, penny and twopence. When a customer had licked the ice cream off the glass, usually with the help of his fingers, it was rinsed in a pail of water and wiped dry with a cloth. Hygiene became a major issue in 1901, when scientists analysed samples of the water used to wash penny licks. In the majority of cases it was found 'to be an evil smelling, thickish and slimy liquid, full of bacteria and sediments, including, of course, saliva from the many

Below: Before the advent of small bricks, sellers used a little 'ice hawk' to spread ice cream between two wafers.

This 1924 ice-cream van is emblazoned with the reassuring legend 'Made under sanitary conditions'. Marco Rea and his relatives were the first Manchester ice-cream family to produce ices in a tiled factory with modern electrical machinery.

The health risks of penny licks were overcome by serving ice cream in edible wafers. Antonio Valvona of Manchester patented a process for making wafer cups in 1902. These little ship-shaped containers are shown in an advertisement of 1911.

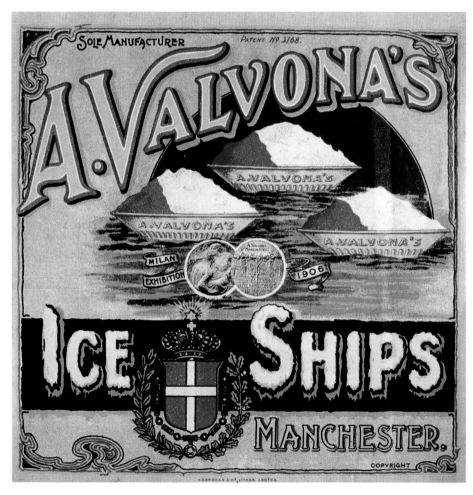

mouths that had touched the glasses during the day'. Ice-cream samples were also subjected to analysis. Many were found to harbour large colonies of harmful bacteria, and foreign bodies such as human hair, coal dust, bed straw, animal hair, fleas and other bugs. As a result, there was a public outcry and a huge drop in ice-cream sales. London County Council passed a regulation that ice cream could not be manufactured in any place used as a living room, or where there was a drain or lavatory. All vendors were also compelled to display the address of manufacture on their handcart, with a fine of 40 shillings (£2) for those who failed to do so. The penny-lick problem was neatly solved by replacing the glasses in the early 1900s with edible wafer ice-cream cups and cones.

By the 1920s cone-shaped wafers were universally used for serving ice cream.

THE GREAT ICE AGE

A S A RESULT of milk and sugar shortages during the First World War, the manufacture of both ice cream and confectionery was banned in 1917. This had a serious short-term effect, but the trade revived energetically after the war. Standards of hygiene improved, larger power-driven machines increased output and many smaller domestic workshops were replaced with well-designed factories. The biggest changes came about as a result of growing American influence on the trade. American-style soda fountains started appearing in Britain before the First World War, the earliest being built in the basement of Selfridges in 1909. During the 1920s and 1930s there was a growing fashion for these establishments. Many Italian families who had started as street traders opened ice-cream parlours, particularly in the seaside resorts. Specialist companies, such as Whitcomb & White of Bloomsbury and Erringtons of Portsmouth, installed fully fitted soda fountains up and down Britain in hotels, dairies and even in Woolworths stores. In the United States ice-cream parlours had spread rapidly during the Prohibition years, and the idea now took firm root in Britain, together with other transatlantic imports such as cocktails and jazz. The latest American-style sundaes, banana splits and other frozen desserts could be consumed in these establishments from fashionable Art Deco *parfait* and sundae glasses.

However, the most enduring influence from across the Atlantic was the adoption of ice-cream manufacture on an industrial scale. In 1922 T. Walls & Sons Ltd, a London sausage-maker, became the first British ice-cream wholesaler with nationwide sales. They imported equipment from the United States and opened a large factory in Acton, west London. In the first year a fleet of ten ice-cream tricycles emblazoned with the famous catchphrase 'Stop me and buy one' was sent out into the London streets to sell directly to the public. By the outbreak of war in 1939 they had 8,500 tricycles and 160 depots throughout Britain. Another major manufacturer at this time was Lyons, who, after a period of selling ices from its well-known teashops, opened a number of ice-cream parlours in London's West End. Proprietary ice-cream powders, which enabled a small business to make up ices by simply

Opposite:
This little girl from a 1920s postcard is enjoying a mult-layered ice cream sundae. A remarkable range of sundaes was consumed in inter-war Britain. With evocative names like Aviation Glide, Ting-a-ling, Come Along Sundae and Lavender Lady, these forgotten delights enjoyed a short-lived popularity until the outbreak of the Second World War.

A sundae was a measure of ice cream flavoured with syrup, crushed fruit and nuts. It was topped with whipped cream or marshmallow. Like the banana split, it had its origins in late-nineteenth-century America.

Above right: New specialist utensils for serving American-style sundaes, parfaits and banana splits emerged in Britain during the 1920s and 1930s.

adding water or milk, became popular during the 1920s and 1930s. The first ices made from emulsifying vegetable fats also appeared at this time.

During the Second World War ice-cream production was severely restricted to save precious milk and sugar. Most of the menfolk of Italian ice-cream families were interned. After the war there was a free-for-all of small back-street traders going into production with little regulation. Public health issues came to the fore again. An outbreak of typhoid in Aberystwyth in 1947, traced to a local ice-cream manufacturer, forced the government to bring in much tighter controls. The new laws made pasteurisation mandatory and all ice-cream factories now had to be registered and inspected by the local authority. Motorised vehicles, some fitted with chimes, became increasingly familiar on British streets throughout the 1950s, 1960s and 1970s, and the ices and lollies purchased from the 'ice-cream lady' became an important element of an evening out at the cinema.

The story of ice cream in the second half of the twentieth century is one of growing industrialisation and mass marketing. The post-war generation was brought up on ices and lollies that were factory-made by

THE GREAT ICE AGE

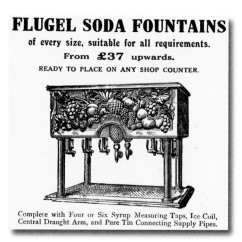

FLUGEL SODA FOUNTAINS
of every size, suitable for all requirements.
From **£37** upwards.
READY TO PLACE ON ANY SHOP COUNTER.

Complete with Four or Six Syrup Measuring Taps, Ice Coil,
Central Draught Arm, and Pure Tin Connecting Supply Pipes.

"**ITALIA**"
ICE CREAM POWDER
D E - L U X E
WITHOUT SUGAR OR EGGS
Specialists in
ICE WAFERS, BISCUITS,
CORNETS, CUPS, Etc.
Write for Samples & Prices.
Thomas Mann, Lᵗᵈ.
BRADFORD,   YORKS.

Far left: Soda
fountains were
never as
widespread in
Britain as they
were in the United
States, but their
popularity rose
significantly during
the inter-war
years.

Left: Instant ice-
cream powders
were very popular
in the inter-war
years.

the big companies. The so-called 'soft-serve' ices, branded in Britain under
the names of Mr Whippy and Mr Softy, were another American import,
first made in 1938 by the Illinois-based company Dairy Queen. They
started to become popular in Britain in the 1960s and were very different
from the full-bodied hand-made ices of the small-scale milk bars and
Italian parlours, or those of the earlier high-class English confectioners.
Higher profit margins were achieved by whipping more air into the mix,
a technique known in the trade as 'overrun'.

Enjoying a 'Choc
Bar' on the way
home from school
in the 1930s.

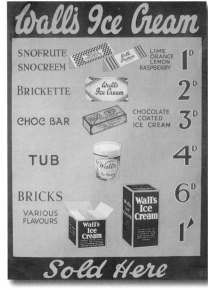

Above: Using American factory methods and aggressive marketing techniques, Walls became the first mass distributor of ices in Britain. Their dark blue tricycles painted with 'Stop me and buy one' were a familiar sight.

Above right: The big firms vied with each other over the names of their new products in the 1930s.

Right: Commonly known as a 'wafer', a small slab of ice cream sandwiched between two wafer biscuits had its origins in the Edwardian period.

The '99', a serving of vanilla ice cream impaled with a chocolate flake, became a popular element of folk culture at this time and was usually served in a cornet. The true origin of this archetypal British confection is a mystery. Cadbury brought out a '99' flake in 1930 specifically for using in ice cream, and the wafer manufacturer Askeys also made a cornet called a '99'. An ice-cream family from Portobello, Edinburgh, claims that the name came from the address of their shop at 99 High Street. Another interesting, though far-fetched, theory is that it was named in honour of the last conscripts of the Italian Alpine Regiment to serve in the First World War. Born in 1899, they were celebrated throughout Italy as *i Ragazzi del '99* – 'the boys of '99'. The chocolate flake is said to symbolise the rakishly angled raven's feather they wore in their distinctive cap, the *capello alpino*.

Ice lollies are also American in origin. They are alleged to have been invented in 1905 by the eleven-year-old Californian Frank Epperson, who left a stirring stick

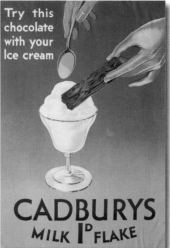

Far left: Walls 'Snofrute' was the first ice lolly to be enjoyed by English children. Like the popular 'Choc Bar', it was of American origin. Chocolate-coated ice-cream bars first appeared in the United States in 1921 under the brand-name 'Eskimo Pie'.

Left: The chocolate flake or '99' has a mysterious history. Before it came to be served in a cone, it was used to garnish sundae cups, as in this 1930s advertisement.

An evening at the 'pictures' was not complete without an ice cream consumed from a cardboard 'tub' with a small wooden spoon.

53

Above: Ice-cream vans first appeared on British streets in the 1920s. The earliest, like this one from the 1930s, were modelled on the decorated horse-drawn carts.

Below: During the Second World War many male Italian ice-cream sellers in Britain were interned. When peace returned, some families, like the Persellis of Manchester, managed to re-establish their own businesses, but others were forced into selling well-known brands under licence.

"NOT BLOOMIN' LIKELY!"

COOL DOWN with a LOVELY ICE

Producers of saucy seaside postcards were quick to exploit the rich supply of innuendos provided by ice cream; 1960s.

in a glass of fruit soda on his porch overnight and woke in the morning to find it completely frozen. In later life he went on to market his discovery, first under the brand-name of 'Epsicle', and then in 1924 he patented it as the celebrated 'Popsicle'. The idea was introduced to Britain later in the 1920s

An archetypal ice cream van from the early 1960s. The body and interior of this 1961 Bedford CA van were designed and fitted by Remo di Mascio of Coventry for Mrs Christine Cox (nee Altobelli) and her husband George. It was still in service in 1995 when the couple retired.

'Raspberry Splits',
'Mivvis' and other
lollies popular in
the 1960s were
miniature re-
creations of the
Victorian bombe
surprise, a frozen
dessert with fruit
water ice on the
outside concealing
ice cream within.

by Walls, who marketed the United Kingdom's first ice lolly under the brand-name 'Snofrute'. A whole range of ices on sticks gradually emerged on the market. Some were made in novelty shapes, such as the 'Archie Andrews', moulded in the form of a famous ventriloquist's dummy. Another old favourite was the 'Mivvi', made by Lyons Maid, its fruit-flavoured exterior concealing an ice-cream centre, rather like a Victorian *bombe surprise* on a stick. The 'Fab', also launched by Lyons in 1967, became a popular brand specifically aimed at young girls. It consisted of stripes of vanilla and strawberry ice, with a chocolate-flavour coating sprinkled with 'hundreds and thousands'.

In contrast to the wide range of flavours offered by Georgian and Victorian confectioners, most English retailers of ices in the first sixty years of the twentieth century stocked a limited range – very often just vanilla. During the 1960s this started to change and a number of ice-cream shops, such as Dayvilles of the Finchley Road and Marine Ices of Chalk Farm, both in London, influenced by Italian *gelaterie* and American ice-cream parlours, started to offer a much wider choice.

Nowadays, the market is dominated by a few industrial giants such as Unilever, and most of the ice cream consumed in Britain is mass-produced. The well-known ice-cream champion Robin Weir, concerned by the artificial flavourings and other additives he discovered his children were consuming in factory-made ices, has passionately advocated that we return to making 'real' ice cream at home. With the wide range of electrical ice-cream makers now on the market, this has never been easier.

Pop Art on the street. This 1981 Bedford HA (Viva) van has been designed and fitted in the style of the Batman television series of the period.

CHRONOLOGY

2000 BC – Ice storage cellars built at Ur on the banks of the Euphrates in Mesopotamia.

325 BC – Alexander the Great orders ice storage pits to be built in the Indian city of Petra.

280 BC – The Greek poet Theocritus describes a chilled refreshment in his poem 'The Cyclops'.

90 AD – Pliny the Younger describes a kind of chilled porridge called 'halica' made with oats, wine and honey and cooled with snow.

1242 – An early description of artificial freezing using alum and water in the Islamic physician Ibn Abi Usabi's book *Kitab Uyan al Anba fi Tabqat al-Atibba*.

1530 – The earliest European description of artificial freezing in Marco Antonio Zimara's *Problemata Aristoteles*.

1589 – The Neapolitan alchemist Giovanni Battista della Porta publishes Magia Naturalis, in which he describes a successful experiment in freezing wine with snow and saltpetre.

1619 – First ice house built in Britain in Greenwich Park by order of James I.

1625 – The Italian scalco, or house steward, Antonio Fraguli describes a feast in which pyramids of ice containing fruits were used as table centrepieces.

1662 – Water ices probably served to Louis XIV at Versailles by the limonadier Audiger.

1665 – Earliest surviving recipe for ice cream in the handwritten recipe book of Lady Anne Fanshawe.

A miniature pineapple garnishing ice partially removed from a 19th century pewter mould.

1671 – Ice cream served to Charles II at a garter feast in St George's Hall, Windsor Castle.

1674 – The earliest printed recipe for a water ice in L'Emery's *Recueil de Curiositez Rares et Nouvelles*.

1676 – Pierre Bana in *L'usage de glace, de la neige et du froid* describes how the people of Italy froze a mixture of fruit, cream and sugar with snow and saltpetre.

1686 – The Sicilian café proprietor Francesco Procopio del Coltelli serves ices in his new enterprise the Café Le Procope in the Rue de l'Ancienne in Paris.

1694 – The Neapolitan food writer Francesco Latini publishes the earliest Neapolitan recipes for ices in *Lo Scalco alla Moderna*.

1690s – The earliest record of vanilla being used to flavour an ice is published in the anonymous Neapolitan booklet *Breve e Nuovo Modo de farsi ogni sorte di Sorbette con facilità*.

1718 – The earliest recipe for an ice cream in an English printed book appears in Mrs Mary Eales' *Receipts*. Eales claims to have sold confectionery to the court of Queen Anne.

1759 – The Turin confectioner Domenico Negri opens his shop at the Sign of the Pineapple in Berkeley Square London, from where he sells a wide range of Italian ices.

1789 – Frederick Nutt, a former apprentice to Negri, publishes *The Complete Confectioner*, with extensive chapters on ice creams and water ices.

1824 – John Conrade Cooke, an English confectioner, publishes the earliest full recipe for what would later become Baked Alaska in his book *Cookery and Confectionery*. Cooke instructs his readers to cover a moulded ice cream in meringue and bake it in the oven.

1843 – Thomas Masters patents the first English ice cream machine.

1846 – Charles Elme Francatelli, formerly *chef de cuisine* to Queen Victoria, publishes the first recipe in English that involves putting ice cream in a wafer cone.

1850 – Henry Mayhew describes the first itinerant vendors of ice cream hawking their wares on the streets of London.

1851 – The Swiss-Italian ice cream maker Carlo Gatti opens a shop in Holborn. Gatti's business booms and he becomes the most important ice importer in London, shipping in large cargos of clean ice from Norway.

1894 – Marshall issues her second ice cream book, *Fancy Ices*, which contains numerous recipes for intricate moulded ice puddings and other frozen desserts. At this time Mrs Marshall also suggests freezing ice cream by means of liquid oxygen.

1902 – Antonio Valvona of Manchester patents an edible wafer cup for serving ice cream.

1917 – The production and sale of ice cream is banned by the Ministry of Food because of wartime shortages of dairy products.

1921 – J. Lyons and Company opens a factory at Cadby Hall to supply ice cream to their tea shops. Their ices are marketed under the name Lyons Maid. Their Polar Maid ice cream was available in vanilla and strawberry flavours.

1922 – T. Walls and Sons Ltd start selling their factory-made ices on the streets from tricycles. In the same year they are taken over by Lever Brothers, destined to become Unilever, now the largest manufacturer of ice cream products in the world.

1924 – The Eldorado ice cream company set up in London.

1926 – Walls introduce the 'Snofrute', a fruit-flavoured water ice in a triangular section cardboard pack, effectively Britain's first ice lolly. It was priced at 1d.

1942 – The government puts a total ban on the manufacture of ice cream products due to the Second World War. Walls' fleet of tricycles is called into national service, fitted with walkie talkie radios and used to train Wrens in ground control tactics.

1955 – Walls launches an orange-flavoured ice lolly called 'Fruitie', which was aimed at the British cinema goer.

1957 – Lyons opens a new factory at Bridge Park in Middlesex.

1959 – Lyons equips some of its vans with the new 'soft serve' ice cream and purchase the exclusive rights to distribute the American brand Mr Softee, in the UK.

1962 – Following the success of Lyons and its fleet of Mr Softee vans, Walls becomes half-owner of Forte's Mr Whippy soft serve business.

1964 – Walls launches the 'Cornetto'.

1974 – Lyons Maid is taken over by Nestlé.

1982 – Walls launches its popular ice-cream gateau, the 'Viennetta'.

1987 – Walls UK inaugurates its range of popular 'Magnum' chocolate ices.

1989 – The confectionery company Mars breaks into the ice-cream business with a frozen version of its iconic Mars bar.

1990s – Thicker, premium-style ice creams marketed by companies like Häagen-Dazs and Ben and Jerry's come back into fashion. There is also a resurgence of so-called 'artisan ices' and a growth of farm-based dairies producing 'traditional farmhouse' ice cream from their own milk.

2000 – Unilever take over the American ice cream business Ben and Jerry's for $326 million.

SOME GEORGIAN ICE CREAMS TO TRY YOURSELF

These excellent ice recipes were published by the London confectioner Frederick Nutt in *The Complete Confectioner* (London: 1789). His hand-written recipes are reproduced on page 14. For clarity the same recipes are reproduced below.

Nutt advocated the use of syrup to sweeten his ices. This can easily be replicated in the following way: bring a litre of water to the boil; remove it from the heat as soon as it boils and dissolve in it a kilogram of white granulated sugar by constantly stirring; when every grain of sugar has dissolved, store the syrup in a jar or bottle in the refrigerator until required.

Note: A 'gill' is a quarter of a pint – 5 fluid ounces. Use whipping cream in all of these recipes. Make the ice-cream mixtures as below and freeze in an electrical ice-cream machine

NO. 122: BURNT ICE CREAM

Take six eggs, one gill of syrup and one pint of cream; boil it over the fire until it becomes thick; then have two ounces of powdered sugar in another stewpan and put it over the fire; let it burn till it melts, stirring it all the time and when you see it is all burnt of a fine brown, pour the other in, mix it quickly, pass it through a sieve, and freeze it.

NB: when Nutt uses the term boil, he means to simmer gently. Make sure that you do not let the caramel burn to a dark brown. A pale brown is perfect.

An ice pudding in the form of a beehive surrounded by its garnishing ices – c. 1880.

NO. 123: MILLEFRUIT ICE CREAM

Take two gills of syrup, squeeze three lemons, put in a pint of cream, and freeze it; cut some lemon peel, a little orange peel, and a little angelica into small pieces. When it is frozen ready to put into the moulds, put in your sweetmeats with a little cochineal; mix your ingredients well but not the cochineal as it must appear only here and there a little red, then put it into the mould.

NB: by lemon and orange peel, the author means candied or preserved peel, not fresh peel. He instructs us to put the ice cream into moulds, but this is not necessary.

NO. 124: FRESH CURRANT ICE CREAM

Take one pint of currants, pass them through a sieve with five ounces of powdered sugar and a pint of cream, then freeze it.

NB: by currants the author means fresh redcurrants, though this delicious ice can also be made with blackcurrants or whitecurrants.

NO. 125: BURNT ALMOND ICE CREAM

This is done in the same manner as the burnt filbert ice cream.

NB: Nutt gives a recipe for burnt filbert (hazelnut) ice cream in another part of his book:

NO. 144: BURNT FILBERT ICE CREAM

Roast some Barcelona nuts well in the oven, and pound them a little with some cream; put four eggs into a stewpan, with one pint of cream and two gills of syrup; boil it till it grows thick, pass it through a sieve and freeze it; then mix your filberts with it before you put it into your moulds.

NB: Barcelona nuts is an old term for hazel nuts.

NO. 126: CEDRATY ICE CREAM

Take two large spoonfuls of essence of cedraty, put it in a basin, squeeze in three lemons and add one pint of cream; observe that all the essence is melted, then pass through a sieve and freeze it.

NB: Cedraty are citrons. An essence was made from the peel of these large, bitter citrus fruits by steeping them in syrup until it became very strong with their flavour. Fresh citrons can sometimes be purchased from Bangladeshi and Indian grocery shops.

A water ice in the form of a basket of eggs made from an 1880s mould. The eggs are flavoured and coloured with coffee.

NO. 127: PARMESAN CHEESE ICE CREAM

Take six eggs, half a pint of syrup and a pint of cream; put them into a stewpan and boil them until it begins to thicken; then rasp three ounces of parmesan cheese, mix and pass them through a sieve, and freeze it.

NB: Though very rich, this is an extraordinary ice cream. Do not boil the mixture in the modern sense, but just gently simmer it until it starts to form a custard.

NO. 128: DAMSON ICE CREAM

Take three ounces of preserved damsons, pound them and break the stones of them, put them into a basin, squeeze in two lemons, and a pint of cream; pass them through a sieve and freeze it.

NB: Nutt intends us to mix the crushed kernels of the damson stones into the ice cream mixture. By preserved damsons, he means damsons in syrup. This is why there is no sugar or syrup in this recipe.

FURTHER READING

Clarke, C. *The Science of Ice Cream*. Royal Society of Chemistry, 2004.

Crowhurst, Basil. *A History of the British Ice Cream Industry*. Food Trade Press, 2000.

David, Elizabeth. *Harvest of the Cold Months*. Michael Joseph, 1994.

Krensky, Stephen. *Scoop after Scoop – A History of Ice Cream*. Atheneum, 1986.

Quinzio, Jerri. *Of Sugar and Snow*. University of California Press, 2009.

Reinders, Pim. *Licks, Sticks and Bricks – A World History of Ice Cream*. Unilever, 1999.

Riley, Gillian. *The Oxford Companion to Italian Food*. OUP, 2007.

Sponza, Lucio. *Italian Immigrants in Nineteenth Century Britain: Realities and Images*. Leicester University Press, 1988.

Weir, Robin and Caroline. *Ice Cream, Gelato and Sorbet*. Grub Street, 2010.

Wheaton, Barbara. *Victorian Ices and Ice Cream*. Macmillan, 1985.

PLACES TO VISIT

Brodsworth Hall and Gardens, Brodsworth, Doncaster, South Yorkshire DN5 7XJ. Telephone: 01302 724969.
Website: www.english-heritage.org.uk/brodsworthhall
Victorian kitchen with ice-cream-making equipment.

Callendar House, Callendar Park, Falkirk FK1 1YR. Telephone: 01324 503770. Website: www.falkirk.gov.uk Working Georgian kitchen with period ice-cream-making demonstrations during the summer.

The London Canal and Ice Cream Museum, 12–13 New Wharf Road, London N1 9RT. Telephone: 020 7713 0836.
Website: www.canalmuseum.org.uk
The site of one of Carlo Gatti's ice wells.

Petworth House, Petworth, West Sussex GU28 0AE.
Telephone: 01798 343929. Website: www.nationaltrust.org.uk
Victorian kitchen with good examples of nineteenth-century ice-cream-making equipment and moulds.

The Royal Pavilion, 4/5 Pavilion Buildings, Brighton BN1 1EE.
Telephone: 03000 290900.
Website: www.brighton–hove rpml. org.uk/RoyalPavilion
Some ice-cream moulds in the kitchen display of copper.

York Castle Museum, Eye of York, York YO1 9RY. Telephone: 01904 687687.
Website: www.yorkcastlemuseum.org.uk
A good collection of pewter ice-cream moulds.

INDEX